Tudor homes

Fiona Reynoldson

Read the introduction to this book first. You can then read any of the chapters which you find interesting. Chapter 12 may be particularly useful to you.

The basic facts are given in big print, and more detailed information is in smaller print.

Contents

1 Introduction

At the beginning of Tudor times most houses in England were built in a simple way. They had a hall or main room with a fire, around which everyone gathered to eat and talk.

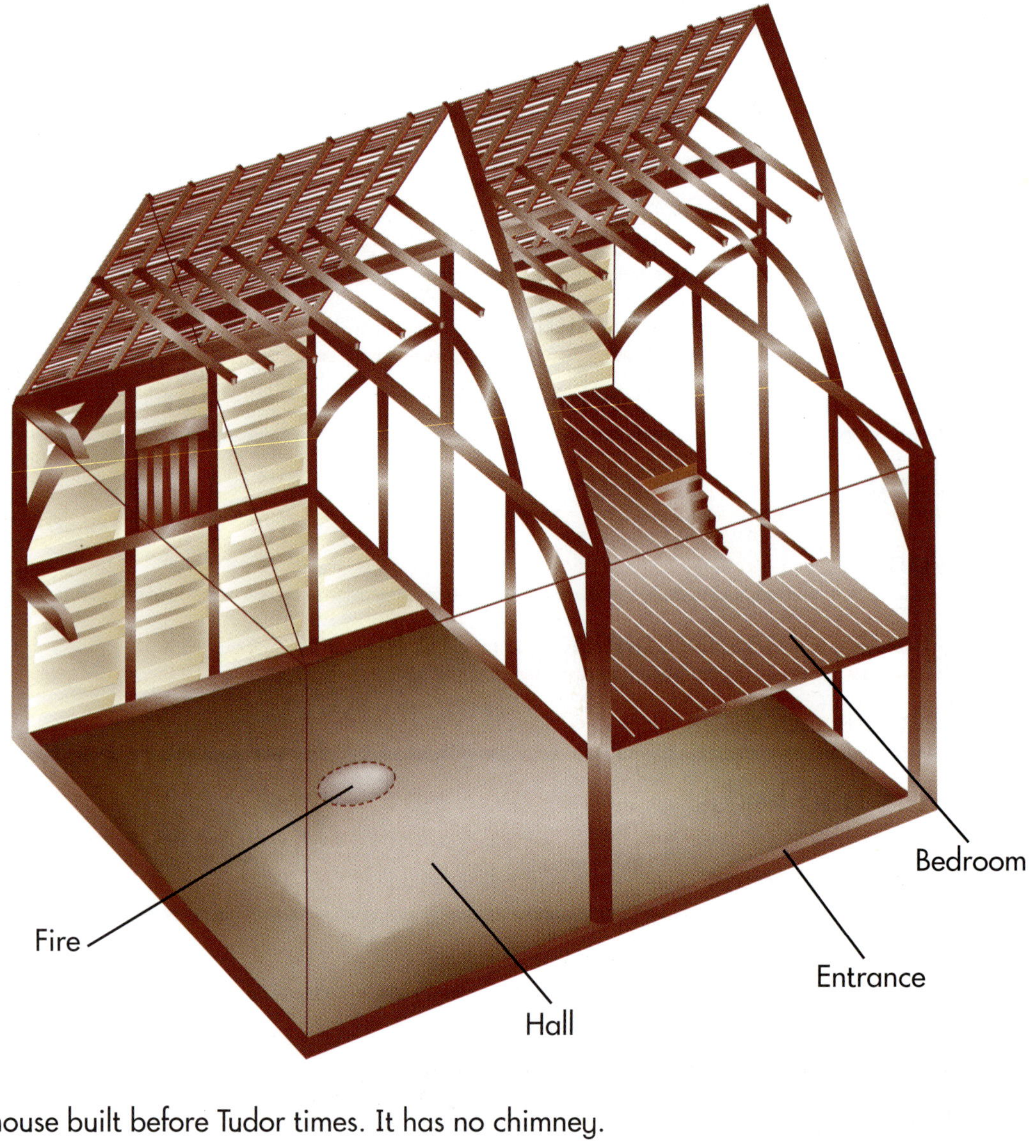

A house built before Tudor times. It has no chimney.

Most houses, especially those in the country, were built in a simple way before Tudor times. The hall was the main room of the house. The fire was in the middle of the hall. There was no ceiling. The smoke from the fire went out through a hole at the end of the roof.

Some rich people in towns and in the countryside built houses that had fireplaces, chimneys and separate rooms even in the Middle Ages. However, it was only in Tudor times that chimneys became available for the ordinary people. It made a great change to their lives. New houses were built with chimneys and older houses often had a chimney added. This meant that the house could be divided up into a number of rooms because more than one room could be heated with a fire.

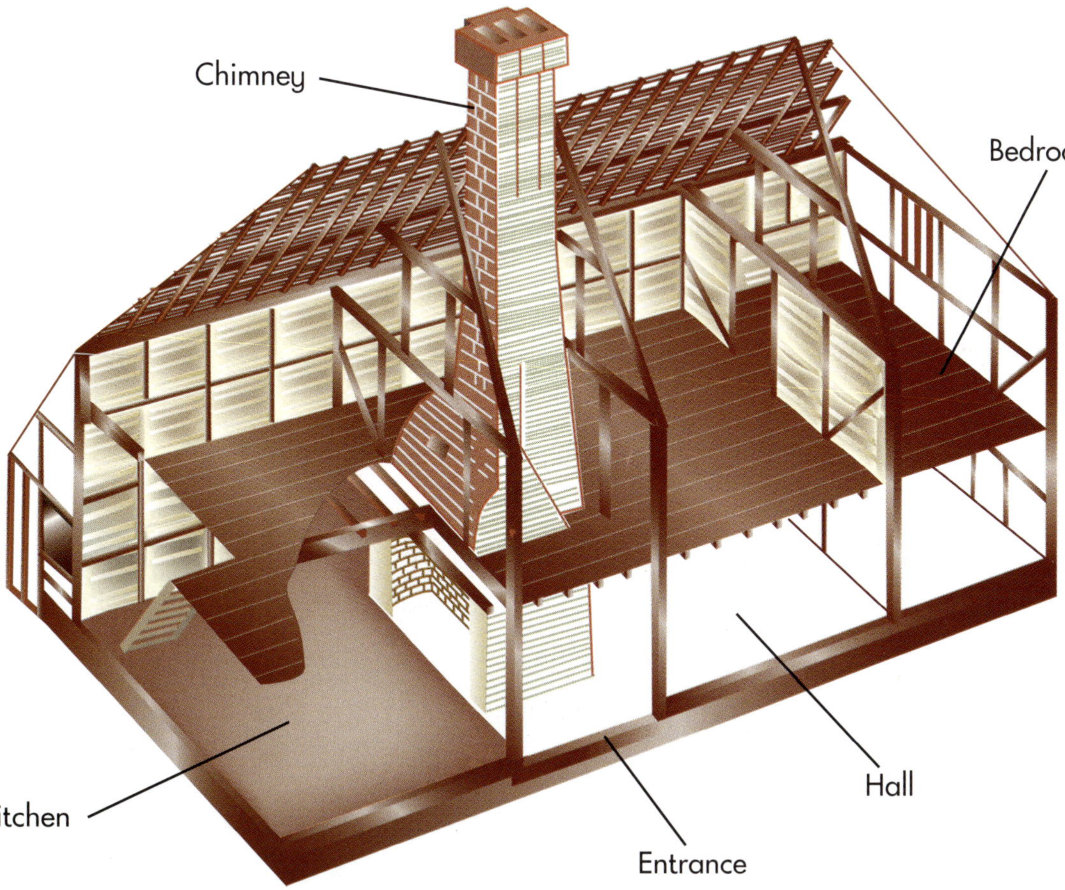

This drawing is of a farmhouse called Pendean which was built in Tudor times. It has a large chimney in the middle of the house.

2 The importance of chimneys and curfews

Before they had chimneys people just used curfews over the fire in the middle of the room. Curfew means 'cover fire'. When it was time to go to bed, people covered the fire to make it safe without putting the fire out. When they woke up they would take the curfew off and the room would be warmed again.

In this picture the curfew is the upside down bowl to the right of the fire.

By Tudor times chimneys were becoming very popular. Having a chimney meant that the fires were enclosed in fireplaces. People could have more than one fireplace and in more than one room. The fires could be controlled more easily and there was less danger of fire spreading. People could live in separate rooms, not just in one big room, and they could still keep warm. In fact, they could keep warmer because the rooms were smaller and often had ceilings.

At the side of the chimney there was often a small oven for baking bread but the main cooking was still done in a pot, called a cauldron, over the fire.

The new chimneys were built either in the middle of the house or on an end wall. The chimney meant that two rooms downstairs could each have a fireplace. Both fires used the same chimney. One other great advantage of having a chimney was that ceilings could be put in because the smoke from the fire no longer had to go out of a hole in the roof.

All this made life much more comfortable. A warm, brick chimney went right up through the floors of the house. Even the upstairs rooms could have fireplaces.

Pendean was a new house in Tudor times and was more comfortable than the older ones, but it still did not have glass in the windows so it could get very cold.

Philip Wyot kept a diary at this time and this is what he wrote one December night in 1590:

"On Sunday at night, a great snow fell so cold that bread and all moist things were frozen in the house."

However, things were going to get better in later Tudor times for those people who could afford glass in their windows as well as chimneys.

3 Big houses and glass windows

Some rich people still lived in castles but by Tudor times, England was more peaceful.

Rich men and women began to build themselves big, comfortable homes with glass in the windows instead of having open holes.

The Wars of the Roses ended in 1485. King Henry VII became the first Tudor king. For the next hundred years England, as a whole, grew more peaceful and more prosperous. New lands were discovered overseas and English merchants traded in all sorts of goods such as wine, timber, fish, wool, furs, spices and silks. At home, the population grew so farmers and landowners made more money from selling their produce to more people.

"Hardwick Hall, more glass than wall"

Bess of Hardwick came from an ordinary family. She made a great deal of money by marrying wealthy landowners. Each of her husbands died and each time they left her their money. She became the richest woman in England after the queen, Elizabeth I. She also made money by farming, buying and selling land and trading in goods. She used her enormous wealth to build Hardwick Hall in Derbyshire and, because she loved light, she had lots of large, glass windows put in, using lots of glass. This was expensive and very unusual in those days and there was a saying at the time: "Hardwick Hall, more glass than wall".

Hardwick Hall had lots of large glass windows.

4 The design of town houses

Towns were much smaller than they are today but the houses were crowded together along the main street. They usually had large gardens at the back.

Many of the houses in the main street were shops as well as houses.

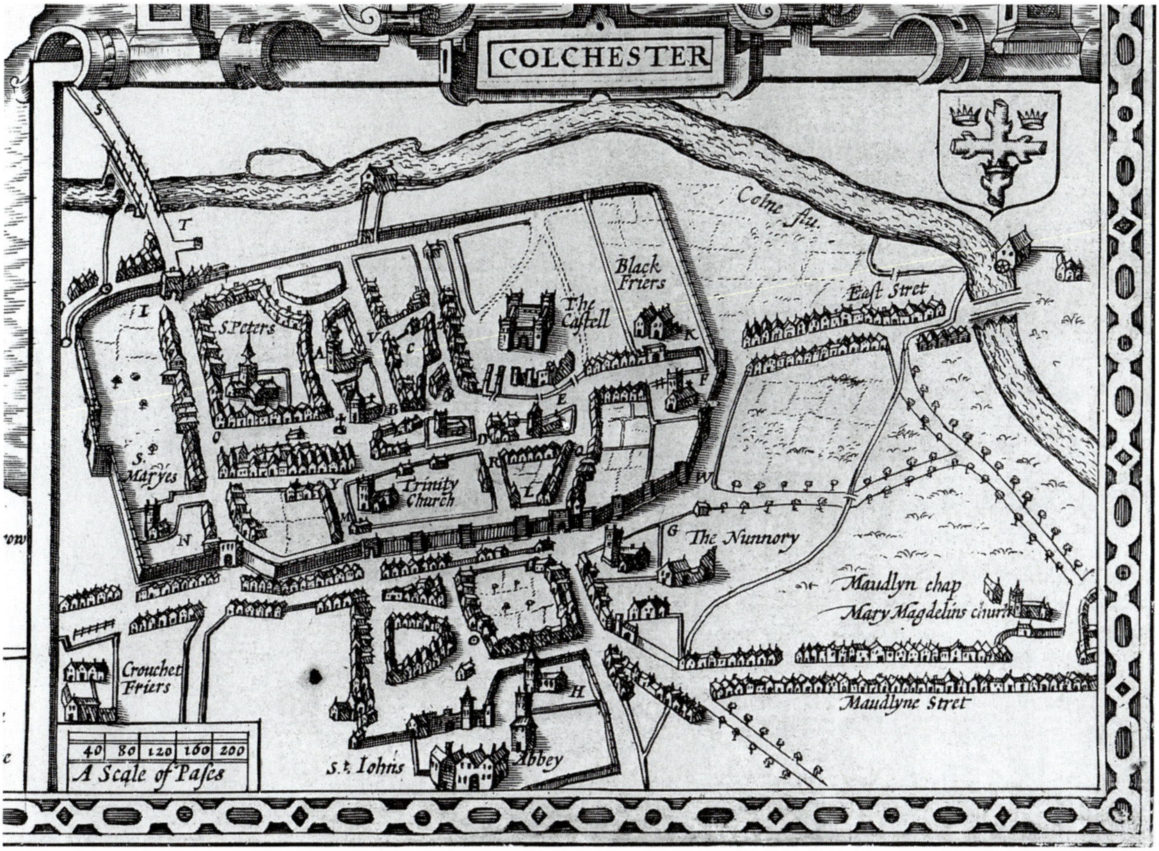

A map of Colchester shows the houses crowded together.

Houses and shops

There was less space in towns than in the country so houses were often three or four storeys high. The ground floor might be a shop with an open front, closed at night with a big shutter. During the day the shutter was let down to make a table to put goods on.

A family business

Behind the open front were workshops. If the shop sold shoes, the shoes were made in the workshop by a master and his apprentices. They were sold at the front of the house, often by the master's wife and daughters.

The family lived on the floors above, and at the back they usually had a garden for growing vegetables and fruit and keeping a pig or perhaps chickens.

A shoemaker's shop.

Building materials

In Tudor times houses were made of whatever was nearby – wood, stone or bricks. In places such as the Cotswolds or Yorkshire there was plenty of stone for houses. However, in London and much of the south, houses were made with timber frames that were filled in with either wattle (woven sticks) and a sort of plaster called daub or with bricks.

The huge timber frames for London houses were often made in Kent or Essex and then shipped to London to be erected there. Once up, the frame was filled in and the roof put on. In many towns there were laws to make people use tiles rather than thatch because fires started so easily in thatched, wooden houses and could spread quickly along the densely packed streets.

Number of floors

In most big towns, such as Exeter, houses were at least three storeys high. In London, rich merchants built houses five storeys high. Part of the building was used for storing the cloth, wine or whatever the merchant dealt in. He and his family lived in the rest of the house.

To make extra room, the houses were often built with a jetty. This was when the first floor came further out than the ground floor. Sometimes the second floor came out even further and in some city streets people in the top windows could shake hands across the street.

5 Inside farmhouses – the hall

The hall was the biggest room in the house. Often it was open to the roof. The fire was in the middle of the floor. The smoke went up to the roof. Then it went along the roof to a hole at one end where it escaped to the air. In the newer houses there was a chimney which must have made the room much less smokey.

People did not have much furniture so there might only have been a couple of stools, a bench, a table and a cupboard.

In the middle of the hall was a fire.

When you went into a Tudor farmhouse you went straight into the hall. This was not just the entrance, it was the living room and dining room too. Here the family ate at a long narrow table, sitting only on one side so that servants could bring food to them easily. The servants ate at the other end of the hall and later in the day, some may have slept around the fire.

There was no glass in the windows but shutters were closed at night to keep out the cold. The only light at night was the light from the fire and from candles. Richer farmers had hangings of wool on the walls for decoration and to keep out the draughts.

During the Tudor period farmhouses were built with chimneys. This meant that houses could have several smaller rooms and families could choose to eat, not in the hall but in a small room, often called the parlour. A parlour was warmer because the fire could warm the whole room easily and it was more private.

A richer farmer's parlour later in the Tudor period.

6 Inside farmhouses – the bedrooms

In many farmhouses the bedrooms could only be reached by climbing a ladder. There might be one or two bedrooms on the first floor. The parents of the family had a large bed and several of the children would sleep in the same room.

A truckle bed under the main bed.

Farmhouses often had two bedrooms upstairs reached by a steep ladder or staircase. The bedrooms were large and the parents and some of their children slept in one of the bedrooms. The main bed was made of a wooden frame with rope strung across it to support a mattress which was stuffed with wool (rich people sometimes had feather mattresses). The bed was closed in with heavy wool curtains which must have helped keep out the draughts that whistled through the cracks around the window shutters.

There was often a truckle bed as well which was stored under the big bed in the day and pulled out at night for one of the children to sleep on. Other children slept on mattresses on the floor.

In the corner of the main bedroom there might be a door to a garde robe (toilet).This was a seat with a hole in it and the waste dropped straight to the ground below. This was very helpful because people did not have to go down the ladder and out into the cold to go to the toilet.

The servants or older children often slept in the other bedroom on mattresses. Hopefully these were wool mattresses and not the straw-filled mattresses that poor people and servants often had.

Bedrooms in rich houses were more comfortable.

7 Kitchens

A poor person's house only had one room so it was the kitchen, the living room and the bedroom for all the family. The cooking was done over the fire in a cauldron. There was no oven so bread was taken to the village baker to be cooked. Rich people had enormous kitchens with at least one large fire for roasting meat and several smaller ovens.

A cauldron over the fire.

A rich person's kitchen in 1570.

By Tudor times, people such as farmers and merchants had larger houses with separate kitchens. The bigger the house, the larger the kitchen to cook for all the family, servants and guests.

People who were better off ate the same vegetables as poorer people but they ate meat and fish as well. They still used cauldrons for cooking but they also often had bread ovens built into the chimney so they could bake their own bread. The loaves were usually the size of small buns. Some people still cooked flat loaves called trenchers which they used as plates to eat off. The juice from the food soaked into the bread and then the trenchers would either be eaten or they would be given to the poor. However, by Tudor times most people were eating off pewter or wooden plates.

Rich people's kitchens were very large. One of the best examples is at Hampton Court Palace which belonged to Henry VIII. Here two meals for 600 people were cooked every day.

Whole oxen, boar and deer were roasted on huge spits in front of the fires. Seven boys were employed to turn the spits so the meat roasted evenly. They were allowed a jug of ale (weak beer) while they worked, but they were not allowed to take their clothes off, however hot it got. The kitchen must have been a very hot place to work. There were not only the great fires but also ovens for baking bread and charcoal-burning stoves for cooking sauces and custard.

All the food was served in big dishes so each person could choose from each dish. No one was expected to eat and drink everything and the left-overs were essential for the servants and the poor people begging at the gate.

This is a list of the food allowed for one rich person on an ordinary day:

One gallon of ale
Two thirds of a pitcher of wine
Meat pottage
Beef
Mutton
Veal or chicken
Rabbit

Heron, cocks, plovers, pigeons
Baked meats (might be sweet)
Fruit
Butter

Part of the kitchen at Henry VIII's palace at Hampton Court.

8 Servants

Many Tudor homes had servants because there was a lot of work to do. No one paid servants much money. The servants lived in the house and in some ways were part of the family.

A servant girl.

In most houses servants lived in the house and ate in the same room as the family. On a farm, there were outdoor servants as well as indoor servants. In a merchant's house there were apprentices learning the job as well as servants so often there were many people living in one house.

The house itself and the people in it were looked after mainly by women. The mistress of the house saw to getting the food, cooking, cleaning, looking after children and the household's health. She was helped by maidservants who were busy from dawn to dusk.

In Tudor times food was not bought at supermarkets or shops. The women collected herbs and vegetables, ran the dairy, looked after chickens and pigs, preserved food for the winter and cooked for the household.

A demonstration of how women made butter and cheese in the dairy.

One household

John Johnson was a wealthy London merchant. He did so well that he bought a manor house in the country. His wife, Sabine, stayed in the country and ran Glapthorne Manor while John was away on business.

Sabine had a number of servants to help. She had a cook who was paid 21 shillings a year all found. (All found means all her food, clothes and a place to sleep were provided.) The cook took charge of all the baking of bread and brewing of ale as well as cooking each day. There were four other servants. All these servants slept upstairs and worked around the house sweeping, sewing, spinning, mending and washing.

At busy times, such as Christmas when there was feasting and guests staying, local women came in to help too. In the account books, a woman from the village came to help for ten days in December and was paid a penny a day.

9 Religious houses becoming private houses

When Henry VII and Henry VIII were kings there were still many monasteries in England and the Church was very powerful because it owned about a quarter of all the land in England. Many men and women lived in either a monastery, nunnery or some religious house. This was their home. But Henry VIII changed all this.

The ruins of a monastery.

In 1536 Henry VIII decided to close the monasteries and to take their land. Before this time there were about 800 monasteries and other religious houses in England. The biggest religious houses, such as those at Glastonbury and Fountains Abbey, owned and farmed huge amounts of land. Some of the monasteries were very rich though many were small and poor.

The monks and nuns were people who had given up their possessions and devoted their lives to God. They looked after the poor and sick, ran the monastery and its lands. Some monks were poor and worked hard but others had grown so rich that they led an easy life with servants to do their work. When Henry VIII decided to do away with all the monasteries, many people agreed that these religious places had outlived their usefulness. Henry, of course, did very well from all the lands and money he got. He sold the land and buildings to lords and gentlemen who were keen to have more land. They turned the monastery buildings into homes or used the stones to build new houses. Some lovely Tudor houses would not have been built if the old monasteries had not been pulled down.

A great house built after the destruction of the monasteries.

10 Vegetable gardens

Gardens were important for growing vegetables such as beans, onions and peas. A big garden also had an orchard of fruit trees, perhaps some chickens or even a pig in a sty. There might also have been one or two beehives so that people could have honey to sweeten their food.

Many vegetables were grown in Tudor gardens whether the owners were rich or not. There were beans, carrots, onions, leeks, cabbages, garlic, parsley and peas. Most of the vegetables were used to make pottage which was a thick stew cooked all day in a cauldron over the fire. It tasted like a thick vegetable soup and was often flavoured with herbs. This was the food that most Tudor people ate most of the time. Only rich people ate plenty of meat and fish.

The countryside

In Tudor times England was a land of forests and moors. Hundreds of thousands of acres in counties such as Devon, Hampshire, Lancashire and Westmorland were uninhabited and unfarmed. There was plenty of wild land left and wolves still flourished in remote places. On the whole, Tudor people did not like wild land. They had enough of it all around so when they made gardens they liked neat, well planned gardens.

Tidy gardens

Vegetable gardens were laid out neatly. There were paths between the beds and the crops were grown in different beds each year so the soil was not drained of goodness and plant disease was kept down. The big houses had gardeners but for most people on farms or in towns, the vegetable garden was run by the housewife.

Plan of a vegetable garden.

11 Flowers and herbs

The Tudors enjoyed flowers so they grew them in their gardens and picked them to have in the house. They also grew many herbs such as sage, thyme and parsley to flavour their food and to make medicines.

The Tudors grew most of the flowers we grow today though they were often smaller. There were tulips, iris, roses, lily of the valley and daisies.

> Everyone liked sweet smelling flowers and the herbalist John Gerard wrote:
>
> "Dafodils are so sweet that very few are sufficient to perfume a whole chamber *(room)*."

When there were no fresh flowers in winter, dried flowers and herbs such as lavender were sometimes put on the floor among the rushes so that they gave a pleasant smell as they were trodden on. Housewives also dried flower petals and put them in bowls to make sweet-smelling pot pourri to put around the house. Another way to make rooms smell pleasant was to use pomanders (oranges with cloves stuck in them).

Many women made the medicines for their families. They used sage tea for sore throats, feverfew for fevers and headaches, and hops, lavender and valerian to soothe. They grew all these and many other herbs in the garden.

Bowl of pot pourri in a dining room.

12 Historical sources

We know about Tudor homes because some of them still survive, some people wrote about their homes and gardens and artists painted them. Of course, houses do not stay the same for 400 years so the Tudor houses that survive today are different from what they would have been. They have had parts built on and other parts knocked down. They have had new kitchens put in and bathrooms added. Even so, you can still get an idea of what Tudor buildings were like from the many towns where although the houses have changed, the streets follow the same pattern as they did in Tudor times.

However, it is very difficult to know how the poorest people lived. They could not read or write so they did not leave diaries or letters or books telling us about their homes. Nor did anyone else write much about them. Just as artists mostly painted rich people in lovely clothes, so writers wrote about big houses and the rich people who lived in them. What makes it even more difficult is that the homes or cottages of poor Tudor people have not survived. They were made of sticks and mud and thatch and they soon fell apart. Often the houses we think of as Tudor cottages were, in fact, the homes of wealthy farmers.

Tudor houses which have now been made into shops.

Glossary

Ale	Ale is a weak beer.
Apprentice	An apprentice is a young person learning to do a job by working with a master and being taught by the master.
Cauldron	A cauldron is a pot for cooking in over a fire.
Curfew	A curfew is a cover, usually made of pottery, which was put over a fire to make it safe without putting it out.
Daub	Daub is the mud mixture used to fill in between wattle sticks.
Garde robe	A garde robe is a lavatory.
Hangings	Hangings are pieces of material used either to cover windows, walls or to go around beds.
Jetty	A jetty is one storey of a house that sticks out further than the one below.
Monastery	A monastery is a religious house where monks live and work.
Mutton	Mutton is the meat of a sheep.
Nunnery	A nunnery is a religious house where nuns live and work.
Pitcher	A pitcher is a jug or container for holding wine or ale.
Plover	A plover is a wild bird eaten in Tudor times.
Pot pourri	Pot pourri is a mixture of dried, scented flower petals.
Pottage	Pottage is a thick vegetable stew, sometimes with some meat in it.
Shutter	A shutter is a wooden covering for a window.
Trencher	A trencher is a flat, circular plate often made of bread.
Truckle bed	A truckle bed is a small, low bed on wheels that was stored under a large bed during the day.
Wattle	Wattle is made of sticks made from wood such as hazel that were woven to make walls.

Further information

Further reading

The Tudors and Stuarts by Philip Sauvain, Wayland 1995
A good, general book with good pictures.

Food and Feasts in Tudor Times by Richard Balkwill, Wayland 1995
Very good pictures about food for the rich and the poor with meals and recipes to cook.

Hampton Court booklet on 'The Tudor Kitchen'
Detailed pictures of Henry VIII's kitchen at Hampton Court Palace.

The Bayleaf Farmstead, Weald and Downland Museum
A great deal of detail about a farmhouse and farm in medieval and Tudor times.

The Making of the United Kingdom by Fiona Reynoldson and David Taylor, Heinemann 1998
Detail on the reigns of the kings and queens, plus a look at life in towns and in the country.

Tudor Life by Sallie Purkis, Addison Wesley Longman 1995

Your Tudor Locality by Sallie Purkis, Addison Wesley Longman 1995

Places to visit

Weald and Downland Open Air Museum, Chichester
Opening times vary.

Hampton Court Kitchens, Hampton Court, London
Open: Monday to Sunday 9.30 a.m. – 6.00 p.m.

Index